CYBER ACTOR

With

MARKIE AND MACKLE

Ken Donaldson

Copyright

Note From Your Author

In the true tradition of Markie and Mackle activity books. I am happy
to bring to you a fun activity book with this one a tribute to our state based
cyber actors from the animated world of paper and screen to all members of
the family.

Like all Markie and Mackle custom design themes this book here is no
different in it's approach to provide entertaining fun while learning or
re-learning one of life's greatest skill we all need to either improve or
retain as one of our own key functions in life.

While the human brain is an natural I or (N-I) unlike our computer
counter-part the AI. Human brains when not keep actively trained tend to
loose memory at any age of life.

Inside this magic book of activities is a custom design method to assist with
both memory training for the very young to memory retaining for the times
when we find our-self becoming a little forgetful and just want to sharpen up
the I data storage banks inside our brain too.

As your Author I welcome you to the puzzle box of mind provoking tributes
to some of our national treasures cyber-actors from which Markie and Mackle
have bought together to amuse and entertain your N-I's memory recall functions.

Thank you and Enjoy

Ken Donaldson Author

Hello,
I am Mackle.
You can colour me in
And together we would
like to share with you our tribute
to Cyber Actors.
With pages of activities for you to
solve and share with friend or family
as you seek out answers along
the way.

Prelude

I AM STATE BASED CYBER ACTORS YOU THAT YOU HAVE COME TO
KNOW THROUGH CYBER STREAMING WAVES TO YOU IN ANIMATED
FORMS SHOWN AS BOTH HERO AND VILLAIN AT TIMES WITH MY OWN
POLITICAL AGENDAS HIDDEN IN PLAIN VIEW ON YOUR READING DEVICES
STREAMING AT YOU BOTH DAY AND NIGHT.

AS WITH ALL GOOD PUZZLE MEMORY TESTING ACTIVITIES BOOK.
THE FOLLOWING PAGES HAVE BEEN DESIGNED TO TEST YOUR MEMORY.
BUILD MEMORY RECOGNITION AND DEVELOP YOUR BRAINS NATURAL
THINKING PROCESSES.

EACH PAGE CONTAINS A TRIBUTE TO WELL KNOWN CYBER ACTORS
FOUND ON-SCREENS IN CARTOON ANIMATIONS, MOVIE ANIMATIONS,
WEB PAGES AND OTHER CYBER PORTALS PLUS MAKING APPEARANCES
IN COMIC BOOKS AS WELL AS ADVERTISEMENTS THROUGH
MASS-MEDIA BROADCAST UPON PUBLIC FREE TO AIR DOMAINS.

NOW IF YOU ARE SET LET'S HAVE SOME FUN WITH MEMORY
RECALLING ACTIVITIES DESIGNED TO SHARPEN UP YOUR MEMORY
AND PREVENT THOSE FORGETFULNESS PROBLEMS THE N-I'S FUNCTION
SOMETIMES SUFFERS FROM.

tomorrow
the
world

Contents

ah
ha!

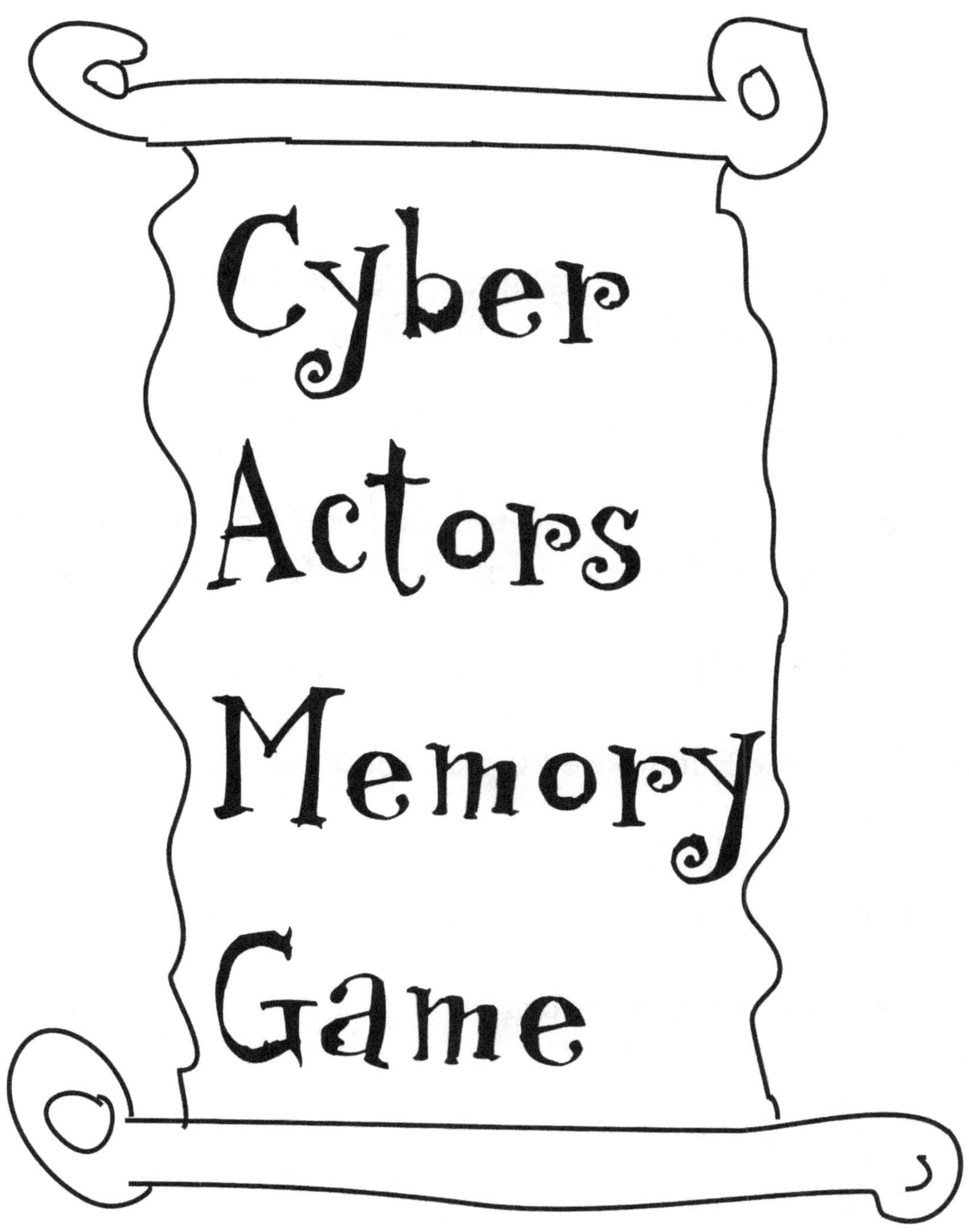

Cyber
Actors
Memory
Game

From among the cyber actors, I came to be best known in life
with an animated film called Steam Boat Wily.

I have always been a favourite with children around the world.

I was one of the founding cyber actors that built an entertainment
empire for one very well known man both in life and even now in death.

One of my greatest role as a cyber actor seen me star in Fantasia

You know me as the State Based Cyber Actor called who?

Write your answer here ___________________

and colour me on on the other page.

Among cyber based actors I have been seen as one of the lovable Villains.

I am often found displaying a self greedy nature I can not help; since I see's it I got to have it. One of my favourite sayings is "It's mine, all mine, mine, mine ,mine I tells ya".

You may often see me in the friendship of a rabbit or a human both of who are also cyber actors too.

Can you guess who I am ______________

Write your answer in the space provided above.

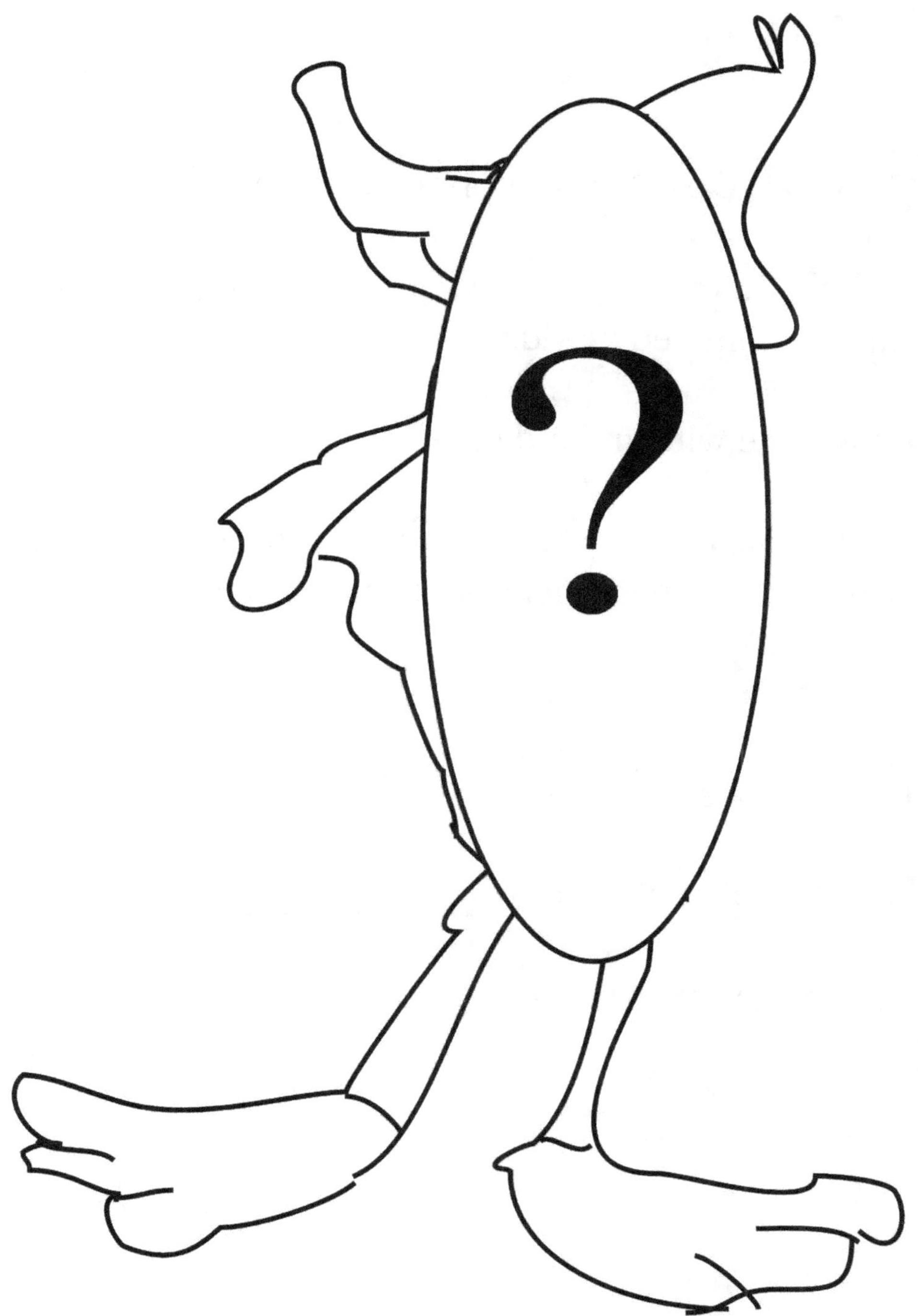

"Yab Dab Do!" You will often hear me shout that.

I would be the oldest of cyber actors if time was a reality in animated worlds.

I have one wife and a daughter.

I am known for my hair-brained schemes that often Fail and get my best friend and I into trouble.

I love to bowl.

I work in a stone quarry.

Which cyber actor am I? ___________________

Write your answer in the space above

From among the villains of cyber actors I am one of
the most devious and despicable villains with only
one thing on my mind.

I love a company called ACME who supply all my
super villain needs in the hunt and capture of my favourite
meal that some how keeps getting away while foiling all
my well planned schemes.

I live in a desert canon.

I have no friends and I am always hungry.

Although I am the villain I am often the victim of the hero.

Who am I? _______________

I am one of the good boy bad boy's of the cyber actors.

I am the eldest son and I live in SpringField.

I go to school riding a skateboard

My best friend is often bullied and I have save him form
getting the pink belly treatment.

I have played both the model role citizen and the bad boy.
But I am good at heart.

I have a sister has a large political voice and sometimes
I am also devilishly presenting a political message with out you
realizing it in many of my performances.

"Hycrumbra" is something I like to say.

Guess which state based cyber actor I am

____

Write your answer in the above space.

Unlike most cyber actors I live under the sea in a pineapple home
Made especially for me.

I work at a fast food restaurant.

I came on the screen in recent times dating back to 1999.

I can b heard in over 55 languages and have a following of
Around 100 million fans.

I am a good guy loved by children mostly under 7 year old.

You might think of me at clean up times after a meal as you wash
the dish, pots and pans.

Who would I be? ___________________

Write your answer on the line provided above.

I love begin a cyber actor sharing weird and fantastical adventures in a world where any is possible as a toon.

Each of my episodes is built around three segments to deliver my message to the viewing world.

I am mostly known by my trademark laugh and open hand gestures.

Which one of the famous cyber actors am I? _____________________.

Write your answer on the line above.

Life is but a road I run it all day.

I love to eat bird seed as a cyber actor my fun is
sticking out my tongue cheekily at my nemesis
who just want to catch and eat me.

My favourite words as "Meep Meep" but often sound
as if I am say "Beep Beep".

I am a good state based cyber actor who is made to do
evil things in order to foil one who wants to eat me all
the time.

Most of my body is blue in colour.

Which cyber actor am I? ______________________

Write your answer on the space above.

Many women love me as a cyber actor who has been broadcasting in both animation and virtual motion film.

A lot of men wish they were me.

I have played both hero and villain with my cyber actors roles.

Though mostly I am the hero of the day saving the world.

My people were not of this world as my birth rite claims.

But I was raise on earth in a place called Smallville.

I first began my acting career in comic books.

I am able to leap tall buildings in a single bound.

Which stated based cyber actor would I be?

_______________________________.

My happy home is Jellystone Park. Where I love to steal them picnic baskets filled with your goodies.

I wear a hat and a tie as a cyber actor who is always smarter than the average bear.

My best friend and partner in crime is always doubting me and thinks I should not do that.

I love to sleep all winter but, when spring comes I am super hunger for some of your apple pie.

I am given the acting role as a loveable villain but if I was real you would run fearing I will eat you too.

Can you guess which cyber actor I am?

____

Write your answer on the line above.

You might think me a super evil genius villain
hell bend on ruling the world with my dumb witted
side kick.

But I am a misunderstood cyber actor who only
wants to have total domination of the world.

My cyber actor character has been chosen as one of
a grumpy rat in appearance.

I have never made it yet to the virtual motion film but
my animated shows delight young and old.

Who do you think my cyber actor character is?

____

Write your answer in the space provided above.

I am a sailor who loves me spinach.

Me gals name is olive and she's a real doll.

When I eats me spinach I have fists of steal and the bigger they are the harder I makes em fall.

I am a cyber actor who is a good guy all round Joe appearing in comics animated and motion film too.

My trademarks are me gal, me spinach and the anchor tattoo on me arm.

Which state based cyber actor am I? _______________.

Write your answer on the line above.

"Nar, what's up Doc" is my most commonly used cyber actor
Trademarks.

I am both the sweet adorable good guy and the evil genius villain
who loves to play nasty tricks on my other state based cyber actor
friends through comic books, animated and virtual motion film.

But the one I love to bully the most is a black duck named Daffy.

One of my most memorable performances was done in
Rabbit Fire, where I really gave daffy some childish bulling.
Ain't I despicable?

Can you guess which cyber actor I am yet? _______________.

Write your answer on the line above.

My world lives in the stone age.

I am a cyber actor who is the voice of reason to my husband
And yet he often does not listen only to learn the hard way.

My best friend's name if Betty.

I am a stay at home wife but, when Betty and I are out we often yell out
our trademark words "Charge it".

I live in a small township called Bedrock.

Therefore I am which cyber actor? ___________________

Write your answer on the line above.

I am a super hero among cyber actors dressed like superman.

I also have special powers that allow me to fly.

My cyber actor form takes on the shape of a mouse.

I am an all round good guy of the animated world and comics.

I fight for justice against all types of villainy as I give a message of right from wrong to my followers.

Who do you think my cyber actor is? _____________________.

Write your answer on the line provided above.

You will have seen me as a laid back easy going dad figure among cyber actors.

My whole world is my son Max a Million who I do everything to try and impress, but, often I mess up a lot.

Guess you could say I am a bit of a goof.

I love Christmas and have often been seen doing starring roles in Christmas animates.

Some of my friends include Donald who is a duck and Mickey Mouse.

I am neither a hero nor a villain but, my son tells me at times I am his hero.

My cyber actor figure is stated based upon the form of a dog.

Do you know who I am? ____________.

Write your answer on the line provided above.

My illustrious cyber acting career brings entertainment
in many forms from toys, books, animated and virtual motion film too.
You name I probably done it.

I am seen in the form of a master mind villainous thief.

I have a love of diamonds but not just any old diamonds.
I love the pink one.

A French detective owes his whole career to me as a bundling
fool name Calouso.

Tell me who I am? _________________.

Write in your answer in the space provided above.

My cyber actor career opened to the world in animation with a short called Dizzy Dishes in the 1930's.

Since then I appeared in Talkartoon before becoming a series of my own. You may not know it but I was originally drawn as a dog character with long floppy ears and great legs.

I became humanized in the cartoon short called Any Rags or was it Mask-A-Raid?

To my name with more than 100 shows under my garter belt including old time radio pantomime and some musical specials. Members of the public criticized me for being too sexy in the 1930's.
All of which added to my greater success as a state based cyber actor.

Have you worked out who I am? _______________________.

Write your answer on the line provided above.

You might know might cyber actor character from Looney Toons.

I crash landed on Earth on July 24 1948.

My first debut was a short called Haredevil Hare.

My uniform is designed after the Roman god of war.
Who was known as?

I love my disintegration ray gun.

My attempts to destroy the earth are often fowled by a black duck.

I am from Mars.

Who would I be? _________________________.

Write in your answer on the line above.

I am like you a normal guy well, mega rich normal guy with a lot of toys to make me a super hero.

I have no special powers but I am highly intelligent and the sole living hare of the Wayne blood line.

I am a caped crusader who began as a cyber actor back in 1939 appearing in comics first, then later in animation and as history passes becoming a star of virtual motion film to.

My stated based cyber actor location is the realm of Gotham City.

My side kick is Robin.

My guardian angel is Alfred.

I tend to live in the shadows of night.

Hence I am who? ___________________.

Write in your answer on the line above.

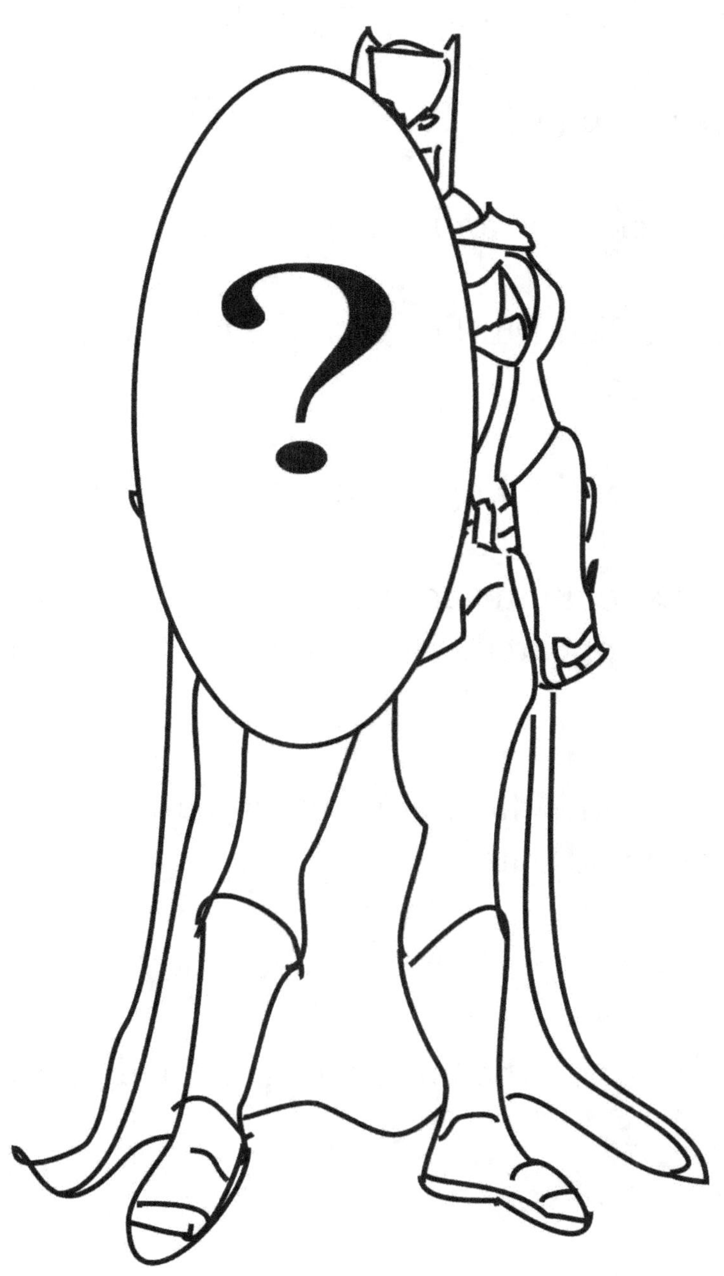

Dastardly deeds is my villainous portrait as a cyber actor.

I love to kidnap women who I leave on train tracks and rob banks.

My pet hates are Penelope and that pigeon.

I have a side kick called Muttley with me in some of my
villainous adventures.

I am the caricature of the English actor Terry-Thomas and professor Fate.

From comic books to animated toons and even virtual
motion film I have appeared. One you may movie you may recall
The Great Race?

Bank robbing, woman kidnapping pigeon hating devious dastardly villain
you love to admire and hate.

I am the stated based cyber actor named who? ___________________.

Write in your answer on the line space provided up top.

Pursed by Dastardly Dick across the annuals of cyber streaming in every form produced from comic, stage and screen. I set out my adventures as the lovable meaning to do no wrong feminine as the only female cast member of wacky races.

My trademark nail polish drying flare of holding my hand out in the breeze while driving may have been copied in the motion film the great race.

My nail polish drying habit often causes the other drivers to think I am giving hand signals which tends to cause great havoc.

My car is a 007 pink nightmare self cleaning terminator equipped with a shampoo foam that often covered my competition.

My sworn enemy is Hooded Claw.

My loyal saviours is the ant hill mob.

Dreamy Peter Perfect is madly in love with me.

I am known as the state based cyber actor who?________________.

Fill in your answer on the line shown.

July 29 in the year 2975 is my birth time as a state based cyber actor.

Raised in an orphanarium as an abandon daughter of two mutant parents named Morris and Munda, I climb up to make a name for myself working with Planet Express flying postage all over the universe.

My crew includes Bender a crazed robot, Phillip J Fry a man shoot out of history past to my time in the future and Nibler.

Other cyber actors I am seen with are Amy Wong, the professor and Doctor Cyberg.

My most notable features are, I have only one eye, a bad childish tempter and a well shaped healthy fit body.

Which female cyber actor am I? _____________________.

Add your answer to the the line shown above.

Portrayed as a dizzy spoiled daughter of wealthy agriculturalist-industrialist whose parents make a living from buggalo the hybrid breed of a buffalo and a bug an animal grown on my home world Mars. Comes the history behind my cyber actor career as a member of Planet Express in which cyber streaming series?

In season six of the series I earn a Ph D in applied physics.

I also find love with an alien named Kif Kroker whom I latter marry and accept the title as Kif's "Fonfon Ru" a little something you call wife.

Tell me from among the female cast of futurama which one am I?
_______________________.

Provide your answer on the line shown above.

ANSWERS

As the cyber actors appear in the book.

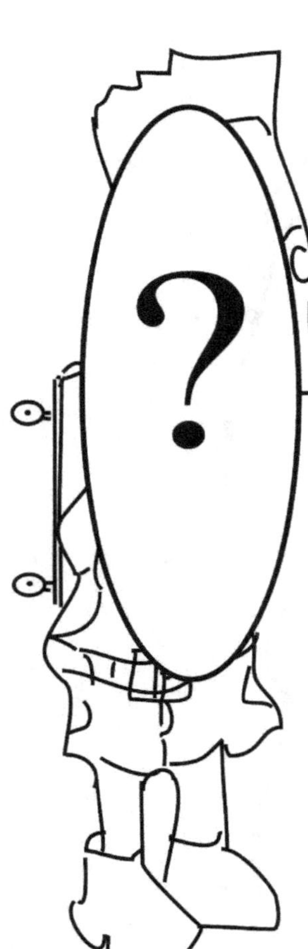

1. Mickey Mouse
2. Duffy Duck
3. Fred Flintstone
4. Coyote
5. Bart Simpson
6. Spongebob Squarepants
7. Felix the Cat
8. Road Runner
9. Superman
10. Yogi Bear
11. The Brain
12. Popeye the sailor man
13. Bugs Bunny
14. Wilma Flintstone
15. Mighty Mouse
16. Goofy
17. Pink Panther
18. Betty Bop
19. Marvin the Martian
20. Batman
21. Dick Dastardly also known as Dastardly Dan
22. Penelope Pitstop
23. Turanga Leela
24. Amy Wong

NOTES

During the composing of this section for the series Markie and Mackle educational books. Where empathise have been directed toward key factors building upon the main theme composition of the series built around fun and activity learning resources designed especially for home-schooling needs as well as a an aid for teacher resources.

As such key factors have been notability included to make the memory training program and or re-training of one's own mental thought process not only fun to colour in or test one's knowledge base through a beloved tribute to cyber actors and the artist who over the years brought joy to the billions of readers, radio listeners, televised viewers and online streaming entertainment channels within our human history's evolving realm that is the virtual world within the reality of life as we know it.

Such key points were designed to ensure the novel's composed theme remained intact by honouring our state based cyber actors or characters with the single who am I question at the end of each one that was included in this edition.

This also left open the option to add research questions to possibly increase one's own personal knowledge of the arts industry through external referencing of material sources both online and other places like the local library.

I hope you have had fun challenging your knowledge with the quiz styled trivia activity tad-bits throughout the book while gaining the benefits of strengthening or training your memory data banks to continue enjoying a much better way of life without problems commonly associated due to age like forgetfulness.
I also hope the young ones making use of this book as a memory program to build their life skills in the area to think and learn independently have enjoyed all this book has to offer too.

ISBN:978-1-71672-587-6
Imprint: Lulu.com
Date: 19 July 2020

LEGAL DISCLAIMER

As the author of this special Markie and Mackle customed designed game and educational book I declare the following truths.

1. The workmanship and or intellectual property are derived from myself as the author Ken Donaldson. Solely for the purpose of tributing artist who bough to life a legacy that is part of human history to us all.

2. The animated characters redrawn are the trademans of designer who produced the stated based cyber actors within the realm where the artist lives.

3. This book is a dedication to many of us who still hold fond childhood memories granted through the state based cyber actors used within the pages of this book as both a tribute to their legacy and for the purpose of educational training to strengthen a person mental thought processes.

4. I do not claim ownership of the illustrated reproductions as original works of my own intellectual imaginings and thereby give credit to all artist whose legendary works have been use to contribute to the health and wellness for all ages of society.

5. Therefore I as the author Ken Donaldson accept no responsibility to any claim from any artist or person against the illustrated representations that may resemble designs of fictional characters living or dead produced by any person living or dead for the use of as part of the works contained here within that have been commonly used freely by the public from which I have used to celebrate a tribute to human history from the state base cyber actors made public to the world's entertainment value.

You can also find other titles to add to your collection from https://themousesdiary.com or general reading for main stream public entertainment at https://bookatreasury.com

www.ingramcontent.com/pod-product-compliance
Lightning Source LLC
Chambersburg PA
CBHW081631250726
48657CB00009B/2821